*"The first experience*

*can never be repeated.*

*The first love,*

*the first sunrise,*

*the first South Sea Island,*

*are memories apart,*

*and touched*

*a virginity of sense."*

R.L. Stevenson
*In the South Seas, 1889*

# PACIFIC

## ISLAND

HERBERT
YPMA

THAMES AND HUDSON

PAGES 2–3
*A detail taken from a decorative column in a church on Mauke Island is indicative of the Polynesian love of colour. Pink and green, in particular, are a strongly recurrent combination: green recalls lush shades of verdant nature and pink is the colour of frangipani blossoms.*

PAGES 4–5
*This Waiheke Island beach house started as a simple beach shack, of which the main redeeming quality was the collection of existing Phoenix palms. Built from New Zealand salt box timber, the design is a mechanism for enjoying the surroundings at different times of the year.*

PAGES 6–7
*Costumed in swaying skirts of traditional **Ti** leaves, young Cook Island girls perform in the lyrical style of traditional Polynesian dance. Like the Hawaiian **hula**, these vibrant dances, set to strumming ukuleles, beating drums and a setting sun, tell of legends remembered and retold.*

*To my parents, Carla and Peter, who have given me a more interesting and adventurous life than anyone could possibly hope for.*

British Library Cataloguing-in-Publication Data
A catalogue record for this book is available from the British Library

ISBN 0-500-07015-6

Printed in Singapore

# CONTENTS

# INTRODUCTION

Since Inca legends first told of 'paradise' beyond the Western horizon, the Pacific Islands have held a special fascination for the Western world.

Exotic reports from the first European explorers only served to reinforce the 'seductive myth' that here, perhaps, was the Garden of Eden; ever since the islands of Oceania have retained their place in the popular imagination as the last unspoiled place on earth.

In fact, the South Pacific might not be as ideal as it once was in our shared imagination. European colonization and imported Western standards, moral and otherwise, have, in the space of less than two hundred years, completely changed the original civilization that the first European explorers found. In its place is a watered-down version of the once pure Polynesian culture. Yet, despite all the changes, this group of islands, spread throughout the Pacific, has maintained, and continues to maintain, a distinct and vibrant culture.

Most clichéd images of the South Pacific start and end with white sand beaches, blue lagoons and palm trees. Little is known of the important and varied artistic traditions of these islands and their spiritual significance and even less about the relevance of these traditions and customs to contemporary society. But the fact that the visual culture of the Pacific Islands has received so little coverage makes it all the more fascinating. Polynesia presents the opportunity of a largely unexplored creative domain.

The culture of the islands, the culture of Polynesia, is one of refined simplicity. Devoted to their ancestors through the expression of their arts, the islands of the Pacific are united by an organic, sensuous civilization that promotes harmony with the environment rather than dominance over it. Polynesian culture exemplifies a simpler way of life, an appreciation of the basic elements of sky, land and water and their importance to everyday life. The people of these Pacific isles, both indigenous and descended from the colonizing Europeans, are acutely sensitive to, and protective of, their Pacific domicile. Their focus is on the value of what they have and the importance of preserving it. In modern Polynesia, there is a concerted effort to build on rather than abandon the tenets of Pacific culture. It is fascinating to see that in architecture, art and design, Polynesian influences, whether literal or inferred, are used wherever possible to help to create a contemporary version of an ancient culture.

'Paradise', it's safe to say, is in good hands!

# 1

# INTERIORS

*We are a curious race. We value our privacy, yet given half a chance we are more than prepared to take a good look around our neighbour's house. How people live creates in us an almost intuitive and insatiable curiosity.*

# A DESIGNER'S COTTAGE

## ON THE

# WAITEMATA

## BACKWATER

Diana Firth, a designer trained in industrial design and fine arts, has turned her eye towards Polynesian influences. As we will be seeing in numerous examples illustrated in this book, the interpretation of a culture is an important step in ultimately preserving it. Diana Firth's house, on the Waitemata backwater in New Zealand, is a collection of colours, details, forms and figures that constitute a new yet recognizably Polynesian style.

In the colours of her furniture and her house, in the details of the pool, the patterns forged into her gate, on every surface in fact, it is possible to discern an environment brimming with Polynesian inspiration.

Firth is adamant that Western sophistication is a folly in the Pacific. As she says, 'We have our own sophistication here but it is different from Western standards.' And so it should be. A search for contemporary expression that remains in step with Polynesian culture has taken her into a myriad of disciplines. Some are more successful than others. A make-up and dressing table she designed a few years ago, decorated with sea shells and painted in graphic stripes of black and white, now appears superficial, yet a chaise parked by the side of the swimming pool is a timeless and more substantial example of design that is firmly at home in the Antipodes. The importance of Diana Firth's contribution towards defining a Pacific style is her endless willingness to experiment. Originally a fashion designer, Firth went to Sydney to work in the 'rag trade' before returning to Auckland and diversifying into architecture, furniture and textiles.

Although dedicated to Polynesian culture, she is certainly not a purist. Interested in the art of Native North Americans and recently in the creativity inherent in various religions all over the world, she makes use of all influences that arouse and inspire her. Hindu icons, native American patterns, South Sea colours and Oceanic patterns and images blend into an expression that comprises a distinct signature.

17

Her house is her workshop, beginning with the front door, a complex collage incorporating many different examples of the very Pacific craft of carving. From the staircase banister, a forged example of a recurring Maori pattern, and the fireplace screen, an aluminium interpretation of *tapa* patterns, to the front gate, a mass of metallic symbolism, her home is a continuously evolving display of Polynesian hybrids.

More decorative than intellectual in her approach, Diana Firth fulfils the need in every society to translate unique aspects of a particular culture into ideas that can be introduced to everyday life. Firth's creativity plays a role in the search for contemporary Pacific culture. Colour, pattern and decorative objects define the realm of Diana Firth's design sense. As she herself says, 'I'm not Polynesian, but I feel it.'

"*Tahitians, blessed inhabitants of*

*Oceania's unknown paradises, know only the*

*good things life has to offer.*

*For them, life is singing and loving.*"

Paul Gauguin

PREVIOUS PAGE (16)
*A detail of designer Diana Firth's own front door reveals a passion for all things Polynesian. The highly prized crafts of weaving and carving, local colours and her ubiquitous trademark reference to the sea are all represented and incor-* porated into a personal creative statement which clearly attests to her belonging to the Pacific.

OPPOSITE PAGE
*Diana Firth's individual style and creativity is in evidence throughout the interior and exterior of her house. An out-* door chaise longue of her own design sits at the edge of the colourfully accented pool. The gardens surrounding the pool, contained within paths of broken sea shells, were at least in part inspired by memories of her grandmother's seaside home.

| 1 | 2 | 3 | 4 | 5 | 6 |
|---|---|---|---|---|---|
| 7 | 8 | 9 | 10 | 11 | 12 |
| 13 | 14 | 15 | 16 | 17 | 18 |

PHOTOS IN ORDER OF
APPEARANCE – PREVIOUS PAGES (20–21)

## 1, 3 & 16

*Firth's recent designs reflect her long-standing fascination with religious imagery in art. Her preference for 'people' to be depicted has resulted in an interesting collection of icons, including a Hindu goddess in a South Sea setting and a roundheaded holy man with a splendid moustache.*

## 2

*The choice of pink and green to decorate the widow's peak of her home is inspired by her feeling of belonging to the Pacific. As she says, 'I'm not Polynesian, but I feel it.'*

## 4 & 7

*Details from the elaborate front door contain many references to elements of Pacific culture, such as **Pandanus** weaving, still carried out by the women of Tonga; carving, a strong Maori art tradition; and bold colouring and lettering, as seen in churches throughout the Pacific.*

## 5

*Her place in a Pacific setting is reflected by the trademark sea shells that have been used to adorn the make-up mirror of her own design.*

## 6

*There is a sense of irony and humour to the carving on the front door. **Nau** means welcome and **Mai** means caution.*

## 8, 11 & 12

*References to her own background are mixed with other influences. A love of flowers and memories of her grandmother's garden play an obvious role.*

## 9

*The cast aluminium fireplace screen was inspired by Polynesian and Native American art. The piece is intriguing, welcoming and defiant all at the same time. It seems strangely familiar, even though it is of her creation.*

## 10

*Firth's approach to influences is quite democratic. Even the Christianity imported by missionaries is represented.*

## 13 & 17

*The most pervasive underlying element of Diana Firth's design is a sort of mystical enchantment. Her work is charming and captivating, yet it defies being slotted into any one particular style or movement. This aluminium wall cabinet is a perfect example.*

## 14 & 18

*Graphic patterns taken from various traditional Pacific art forms are used throughout the house. The entry gate features a recurrent wave pattern that repeats inside as the staircase banister and again in the finer curves of the stained-glass windows of the bathroom.*

## 15

*Although newly made to her own design, the Art Deco appearance of the stained glass windows in the bathroom reflects the passion for the exoticism of Africa and Oceania in the early part of this century.*

## Opposite page

*Religious icons, ornaments from the East, Pacific motifs and Indian art are merged in the creative hands of designer Diana Firth to imbue her home on the Waitemata backwater with mystical enchantment.*

# BORA BORA

## URBAN INFLUENCES

### IN

## PARADISE

The French were not the first Europeans to visit Tahiti. Before the aristocratic Jean-Louis Bougainville sailed into one of Tahiti's majestic inlets and dropped anchor, English explorer Samuel Wallis had been and gone.

Wallis, who claimed the island for Great Britain and named it King George Island, stopped only long enough to allow his men to recover from scurvy.

The tales of Captain Bougainville were a different matter altogether. His accounts of his Tahitian experience established the legend of this South Pacific island as the consummate 'paradise' on earth ... a seductive myth that has continued ever since.

Bougainville himself was not altogether convinced. Despite the acclaim he received for having discovered the proverbial Garden of Eden, he suspected, correctly, that Tahitian society was not as simple and idyllic as it first appeared. Sexual customs were, in fact, complex: unmarried women might be promiscuous, but not married ones. Male Tahitians exercised authority tyrannically, made human sacrifices and practised slavery. And they were constantly at war with other islanders, killing all the men and male children taken in battle − helping themselves to hunks of flesh and skin to display as trophies. Even so, Tahiti was about as close to unspoiled civilization as any European had ever come and Bougainville's parting words, recorded in his ship's log, contained a sense of foreboding: 'Farewell, happy and wise people. Remain always as you are now!'

Although Bougainville didn't actually 'discover' Tahiti, he nonetheless claimed it for his Christian Majesty Louis XV. Bougainville had awakened French interest in the Pacific and although clear title to the islands was not resolved with England until 1847, the French never once hesitated in the heartfelt belief that this paradise was meant for them.

Together with their claim to 'paradise' came the responsibility to maintain it as they found it. What nation on earth could have on its collective conscience that it had

'despoiled' the Garden of Eden? Thus, when the Club Med organization, a French concern, proposed building a retreat village on the outlying Tahitian island of Bora Bora, it was faced with the challenge, on the one hand, of catering to spoiled, luxury-craving Westerners, and, on the other, of preserving the simplicity and beguiling innocence of the South Pacific islands and not damaging the fragile, naive beauty of the island. The brief for the design and realization of the village was an almost perfect oxymoron: 'sophisticated simplicity' was what was wanted.

To fulfil such a task, the developers turned to a French designer who has made an international success of being able to combine the naive, raw and unrefined with the urbane and urban. Paris-based Christian Liaigre draws on the influence of tribal and indigenous forms and reduces them down to their bare minimum. In his work one can see the pure forms of Romanian sculptor Brancusi and the definite influences of African and Oceanic tribal artifacts and furniture. Liaigre was thus the right person to carry out the complex task of designing for such a sensitive environmental position. It was, for Club Med, an inspired choice.

For his design for Bora Bora, Liaigre turned to the disciplines of Polynesian culture: to the traditional *fare* (huts) for architectural detailing, to the abundant artifacts of Pacific heritage and to the legacy of vibrant seductive colour as explored by Gauguin.

Throughout this carefully conceived paradise retreat, the design and decoration thoughtfully recall Polynesian ingredients without in any way suggesting a 'theme park' treatment. With typical Parisian aplomb, Liaigre has created an environment that is elegantly spare and, most importantly, appropriate.

The danger with any design in exotic locations is that the project can quickly become a cliché, or worse, a parody of itself. For Club Med Bora Bora, Liaigre has

PREVIOUS PAGE (24)
*Colour, authentic detail and the odd artifact combine to create an appropriate atmosphere. Paris-based designer Christian Liaigre applied his own blend of 'urbane' simplicity to the interior design of a Club Med village on the remote Tahitian island of Bora Bora.*

PREVIOUS PAGES (26–27)
*At the end of the dock the scale of the main building mimics, in* size and grandeur, the traditional Tahitian communal *fare. The appropriately bright colours and thatched roof ensure that, following the original brief, the building responds to a local architectural vernacular.*

OPPOSITE PAGE
*The main area, where guests gather for drinks, dinner or just to relax, combines Oceanic colour (green and blue) and appropriately Pacific detailing, such as* the trumpet conch shells that adorn the walls. This approach is continued with the sea shells set in patterns into the bleached concrete floor and with the furniture design (occasional tables, chairs, stools and chaises that borrow in finish and form from the shapes and finish of Polynesian artifacts). The design of the entire soaring space relies on a sophisticated series of references to the unique locale.*

*"How do! King Tosh!"*

Omai, 1773
The words of the first South Sea Islander to be taken to England, who, when he was
presented to King George III, forgot his carefully rehearsed lines and improvised
… much to the King's delight!

successfully combined modernity with cultural sensitivity. Resisting the temptation to put all the guests in basic huts, he has seen to it that the village does not want for modern conveniences – bathrooms, bars, restaurants – all presented in a tastefully designed form. From the doorknobs to the plates, everything was conceived and designed by Liaigre, borrowing from, and referring to, the extensive creative vocabulary of Polynesian culture. Polynesian artifacts such as lashed timber-handled stone adzes have been reinterpreted into stylish side-tables; conch shells of the kind used traditionally as trumpets have been utilized as decorative objets d'art; and in the bedrooms, woven screens of *Pandanus* have become shutters. Throughout the village, the architecture borrows heavily from traditional elements. From the thatched roofs to the elaborate timber framework, Pacific ingredients and influences are at all times apparent and appropriate. The entire village exhibits elements from the traditional *fare*, such as thatched roofs and pillar construction. Even the spiral, a frequently recurring symbol in all Polynesian design, has surfaced as the leitmotif of the plates.

Yet all this 'design' does not interfere or compete with the magnificent surroundings. The site and the spaces are as open and unencumbered as can be imagined. Bora Bora certainly does not look or feel like a run-of-the-mill four-star hotel on the beach.

"*J.C.* [*Jesus Christ*] *should have appeared in Tahiti.*"

Herman Melville

| 1 | 2 | 3 | 4 |
|---|---|---|---|
| 5 | 6 | 7 | 8 |

# 1

*Throughout the village floors feature a combination of nautical patterns and traditional Polynesian symbols represented by pebbles and shells embedded in bleached concrete.*

# 2

*Liaigre's design discipline extends to virtually every detail, including even the plates. The spiral pattern, in Pacific blue on commercial quality white china, is ubiquitous in Polynesian culture.*

# 3

*An outdoor shower mimics, in a casual, playful manner, the 'lashing' construction of traditional Tahitian fares.*

# 4

*Even the doorhandles did not escape Liaigre's fine eye for detail. The cast bronze fish-form door hardware recalls the recurrent references to fish in the traditional arts of the South Pacific. Liaigre uses clichés without being obvious or predictable.*

# 5

*Following the form of traditional Polynesian chiefs' tools, Liaigre demonstrates his ability to interpret authentic references, together with his inventive and appropriate use of materials.*

# 6

*Here and there, in a totally unobtrusive fashion, Liaigre has introduced some of his previous furniture designs into the overall scheme, as is the case with this chair.*

# 7

*The colour used throughout the 'village' remains within the palette of Polynesian tints. A series of blue pillars are contrasted with yellow walls and the occasional touch of hibiscus red. A knotted root serves as simple decoration.*

# 8

*Liaigre's total design extends to the bedrooms, where the simple treatment of the sloping ceilings and custom-designed bedheads and stools complete the picture. The furniture design is based on traditional Polynesian forms and patterns that occur in varied arts disciplines throughout the Pacific.*

# O

OPPOSITE PAGE

*A wall-relief detail reveals Liaigre's signature: a Brancusi-inspired shape that recurs in many of his designs. The furniture, loosely based on the form of colonial 'plantation' chairs, is upholstered in an appropriate Pacific blue.*

FOLLOWING PAGES (38–39)
*The roof structure of the communal building is a powerful reminder of the attractive strength of traditional Polynesian architecture. Green-and-blue, one of the Pacific's most commonly found colour combinations, has been used to add a touch of vibrancy to the interior.*

FOLLOWING PAGES (40–41)
*A necklace of painted sea shells is a vivid indication of the vibrant colours of the Pacific.*

# MAORI MYTHOLOGY

IN THE

## INNER CITY

In the beginning there was nothing. No gods, no earth, no sky, no sea.

Not, that is, until Papatuanuku (the earth mother) and Ranginui (the sky father) embraced in the realm of night. From their union, seventy children were born, all male: the gods of the Maori. Living in darkness, longing to experience the light of day, the children attempted to loosen their parents' embrace. All of them tried, but only Tane-Mahuta (the god of human creation) was successful. When finally, after much pushing, heaving and swaying, the parents separated, the children experienced *Te Ao Marama*, the realm of being, of light and life – symbolized by the *Takarangi* spiral.

Architect David Howell reinterpreted the powerful aspects of South Pacific legend for the design and decoration of Workshop, an Auckland avant-garde clothing store. Recently converted from an old motorcycle repair shop, the interior deliberately avoids hiding any evidence of its previous life. It's a rough, no-nonsense interior that celebrates its roots both literally and spiritually.

Apart from the most immediate – and obvious – reference to its locale in the Pacific blue painted floor, the most powerful Pacific ingredient is the distinctive spiral mural carved into the walls (the fact that it is carved into the walls is culturally significant in its own right, for carving was a sacred and honoured profession, and the Maori people shared the Polynesian belief that the artist was the vehicle through whom the gods created and communicated). Artist John Reynolds referred to both Maori mythology and Celtic symbols in an effort to create a backdrop of creative and cultural resonance. Of these the *Takarangi* spiral is the most obvious reference.

Representative of the fern pods that grow in dense abundance all over New Zealand, the *Takarangi* spiral is, for the Maoris, the symbol of creation. The unfurling of the pod is symbolic of the start of life and a reflection of its status in the culture is its appearance on all manner of Pacific artifacts. This coiling spiral is also carved into

the back of the Easter Island monoliths and it can be found in the sketches made by the earliest European explorers of facial tattoos. It was carved into the sterns of tribal war canoes and on the gables decorating the entrance to a chief's house. It survives today as a prominent and distinctly Pacific symbol.

Although the co-operation between artist and architect is certainly nothing new, their relationship in terms of Maori culture takes on a different dimension. Art in Polynesian society does not only fulfil an aesthetic role. Its primary function is the representation of ancestors. Sidney Mead, an authority on Maori and Pacific art, has described this unique attachment to art very well. 'Our ancestors are real persons. Though they died generations ago they live in our memories and we live with them for they are an essential part of our identity as Maori individuals. They are anchor points in our genealogies and in our history. Without them we have no social reality.'

The mural for this inner-city shop thus takes on a symbolic *gravitas* that belies its setting. To Western ways mythology, legend, genesis and *Mana* (spiritual prestige) may seem out of place in an environment devised to sell clothing – but it is important to remember that a basic tenet of Polynesian culture is that it does not distinguish between a spiritual world and an actual world. They are seen as one and the same. Paying tribute to one's ancestors is as much an everyday reality as shopping. Therefore for Polynesians it is perfectly logical to combine the two.

## *"He toi whakairo, he mana tangata."*

### *(Where there is artistic excellence, there is human dignity.)*

### Maori proverb

PREVIOUS PAGES (42 & 44–45) *Custom-made hardware designed to display the clothing, juxtaposed here with the texture of the floor surface, introduces the other significant and influential element to have been introduced to Polynesian culture: the Christian faith. The Celtic Cross style of these forged fittings can be seen to be representative of the influence of the English missionaries in the South Pacific*

OPPOSITE PAGE
*Maori people share the Polynesian belief that art is a vehicle for connecting the past with the present. The designs carved into the walls of this clothing shop are a visible symbol of Maori identity and pride, proof that the heritage of Maori art is very much alive. As Sidney Mead, an authority on Pacific art, explains, 'we treat our artwork as people because it represents our ancestors, who for us are real persons.'*

FOLLOWING PAGES (48–49)
*Pacific blue, Maori mythology and Celtic shapes distinguish the design of this converted motorcycle repair shop.*

# AUTHENTICITY

### AND

# SIMPLICITY

### ON A

# FIJIAN ISLAND

Vatulele, a name that means 'Ringing Rock' in Fijian, is the small Pacific island that the team of Henry Crawford and Martin Livingston chose to realize their vision of a retreat that would incorporate the ingredients of 'local culture' in a place of contemporary relevance.

Henry Crawford, an Australian producer of Emmy award-winning television films such as *Against the Wind* and *A Town like Alice*, and Martin Livingston, a fifth-generation European Fijian, had specific ideas about what a place in the South Pacific should be like and, just as importantly, what it shouldn't be like.

Vatulele, a small island just south of the main island of Fiji, has only one village and the local inhabitants fish and farm just enough for their own subsistence. The villagers also make traditional *tapa* cloth from the bark of the mulberry tree. Situated far away from the colonial capital of Nandi, this attractive little island carries on life in a manner not too dissimilar from the time before the white man got here. Crawford and Livingston were determined to keep it that way.

The site for the twelve huts that were ultimately built was leased from a group of native landowners. In keeping with the Polynesian attachment to land, a plan was put forward that would hardly disturb the island's exquisite topography.

In a manner that is now the recommended approach for the future by the Fijian authorities, all materials – sand, timber, structured poles, cement – were imported from the mainland, carefully unloaded and placed by hand. A construction crane never touched the shores of 'Ringing Rock'. Clearing the site took one hundred men armed with nothing more than knives over three months, and ten thousand tons of materials were barged to the beach to be unloaded by hand during the two and a half years of construction.

Very special care was taken to ensure that the palm trees dotted along the beach, defining the island's 'perfect' lagoon, would not be touched. Today the very same palms provide shade for the *bures* that are carefully built between.

*"I never shall meet another spot so suitable to die in. The world actually vanishes here…*

*Man somehow got here, I think about a thousand years ago,*

*and made a society which was on the whole the most successful the world ever saw, because it*

*rested on the solidest possible foundation of no morals at all."*

Henry Adams
Letter to Elizabeth Cameron, 19 April 1881

As one visiting journalist described it, Vatulele is a true 'toes in the sand' island, a Robinson Crusoe fantasy, devoid of all references to Western lifestyle … no telephones, fax machines, cars, paved roads, electricity wires, noise or commotion.

Aesthetically, the same loose and sensuous approach was applied to the style of the design and architecture. It was a search for a style that would feel 'genuine'. It was certainly not the intention to build a second set for *Blue Lagoon*; rather it was Henry and Martin's intention to combine all the best ingredients of Pacific culture into a single expression. For help with this they turned to an American architect based in Santa Fe, of all places. Doug Nelson had come to Henry's attention in a book entitled *Santa Fe Style* and he had admired the way the architect was able to incorporate the cultural signatures of this unique area of New Mexico into contemporary architecture and design. Given the many anthropological similarities between the Polynesians and the Native North Americans it was not such a strange choice; using an American architect from New Mexico was not as exotic or far-fetched as it sounded. Familiarity with the interpretation of south-west American

*"Throughout history,*
*people everywhere have had their own versions of 'paradise',*
*that haven over the horizon*
*where their hearts would find meaning*
*and a measure of peace and contentment."*

Albert Wendt

PREVIOUS PAGE (50)
*The traditional thatched construction, given support by intricately laced timbers, allows heat to rise and dissipate through the loose thatch, keeping the* **bures** *(Fijian bungalows) nice and cool without the need for air conditioning.*

PREVIOUS PAGE (52)
*Vatulele has achieved a style that encapsulates the most attractive qualities of the South Pacific islands. In the construction of the main* **bure**, *where all the meals are served, strangler vines from deceased trees have been preserved and used to adorn the posts supporting the thatched roof.*

OPPOSITE PAGE
*A simple but appropriate combination of ingredients: walls washed in a warm ochre colour; faded terracotta tiles on the floors; traditional Fijian thatched roofs; furniture adorned with brightly coloured 'washed' canvas; and Polynesian artifacts, such as tribal 'war clubs', artfully arranged as wall decoration.*

FOLLOWING PAGES (56–57)
*Custom-made terracotta pots, hand-made by an artist especially for Vatulele, punctuate and decorate the spaces created by the staircase that leads to the library in the main communal* **bure**.

indigenous culture – the use of traditional adobe, and the influence of the arts and crafts of the Navajo – was all valuable experience in helping to determine which aspects of Polynesian culture should be reinterpreted, and more importantly how this should be done.

Following this vernacular approach, the most striking cultural signatures on Vatulele are the traditional Fijian roof structures. Cool and functional, allowing heat to rise and disperse through the loose thatch, these roofs go far beyond the realm of practicality. They are genuine examples of the exquisite capabilities of Pacific craft. Bound together by woven rope, stained in the traditional and distinct Polynesian shades of pink and green, they are inspiring pieces of handiwork that copy the original island methods of roof construction. Little, if anything, has changed. Despite the danger from the cyclones and hurricanes that they are exposed to, the *bures* and their magnificent ceilings are a powerful component of Pacific style.

The ceilings are just the beginning. Throughout the retreat, by imaginative ways and means, Crawford, Livingston and their architect have incorporated aspects of genuine Polynesian culture. Pacific artifacts such as traditional weapons are arranged artistically in the main *bure*, and *tapa* cloth made by the local villagers decorates the walls of each individual villa. A motif, extracted from a typical *tapa* pattern, is utilized as a recurring logo in the floor tiles and other architectural detailing.

But commitment to authenticity has come at a price. Twice to date, a hurricane has flattened the lovely roofs of the *bures* and each time they have been replaced again with this original, labour-intensive version of Fijian architecture.

Vatulele is a trailblazer as a Pacific development project. Within the deliberate confines of its idyllic offerings, it has set the standard by which all tourist projects are now to be judged. Ecologically responsible, culturally sensitive, geographically appropriate – and simple.

PREVIOUS PAGES (58–59)
*Many travellers to the South Seas have commented on the most extraordinary 'golden' sunsets of Fiji. Amidst the countless palms of Vatulele, the effect of the setting sun is quite bewitching, ending in a strong crescendo of pink and startling magenta, which in this image frames one of the twelve beautifully positioned* **bures**.

OPPOSITE PAGE
*The interior of each residential* **bure** *combines a series of diverse Pacific 'ingredients'. Washed canvas upholstery recalls the Polynesian preference for the colour of surrounding nature; a large clump of coral is used as a coffee table; and floor inlays of white and black ceramic triangles mimic the pattern of the locally made* **tapa** *cloth.*

FOLLOWING PAGES (62–63)
*A close working relationship between a fifth-generation European Fijian and an American architect, who had previously worked in Santa Fe, New Mexico, produced a style that harmonizes unobtrusively with the environment. In the service area of the communal* **bure**, *Pacific and Native American influences synthesize beautifully.*

# 1

*Throughout the resort, a triangular pattern, originally found in locally made **tapa** cloth, is used as a decorative device.*

# 2

*Even the furniture, commissioned especially for Vatulele and designed by Doug Nelson and Martin Livingston, continues the triangular decorative motif derived from a **tapa** cloth pattern.*

# 3

*Bougainvillea, planted in custom-made terracotta pots, is another example of the considered and appropriate detailing on Vatulele Island. Bougainville, the aristocratic French explorer after whom this exotic foliage is named, discovered the fast-growing, beautifully coloured creeper in Brazil in 1767 on his way to the South Pacific.*

# 4

*Martin Livingston and Doug Nelson conceived and executed every detail in the design scheme, including these poetically appropriate bronze brackets that hold a hand-rail fashioned from a jungle vine.*

# 5

*Stairs lead to a mezzanine level that houses a small library in the communal **bure** (Fijian bungalow).*

# 6

*The design of each individual **bure** is situated amongst its own group of palm trees, providing shade and privacy. Detailing is continued in the fashion of the main communal **bure**.*

# 7

*The design and construction of a door to a storage area is a reminder of the carefully stacked stone platforms of Easter Island, the **maraes** built by the Maoris and even the stacked stone archways found on Tonga: an example of the cleverly conceived detailing that is 'generic' in the Pacific.*

# 8

*The distinct shade of warm ochre that colours all the **bures** is the result of experimentation. The final shade comes from the idiosyncratic addition of tandoori food-colouring to lime wash.*

# 9

*Pacific authenticity seems unimaginable without the coconut. The true skills of Vatulele's design team are shown in how they were able to deal with clichés – using them subtly and imaginatively, yet not abandoning them altogether.*

# O
PPOSITE PAGE

*Vatulele's chief source of income is the handmade **tapa** cloth. Made from pounding lengths of wet bark with skittle-shaped mallets, then pressing them together to form pieces as large as tablecloths, **tapa** is decorated with traditional patterns and figurations that recur in Polynesian art forms found throughout the Pacific.*

# 2

# ORIGINS

*None of us exists in a vacuum. Everything about us, where we live and how we live, is inextricably linked to how our forebears lived. Connected to our ancestors via distinct forms, patterns, rhythms and shapes, we belong to societies that are in a continuing balancing act between forging forward and looking back. We cannot escape history and tradition.*

# VOYAGERS

# WARRIORS

## CONQUERORS

When Thor Heyerdahl set out in 1954 from the coast of Peru on a roughly constructed raft of balsa wood logs, he was attempting to prove, by voyaging westwards, that the inhabitants of Polynesia had descended from intrepid Peruvians.

Ironically, his voyage, although undoubtedly one of the greatest adventures in modern history, did little to prove his theory that the people of the Pacific originally came from Peru. In fact, like European explorers hundreds of years earlier, his investigation sparked a renewed interest in the isles of Oceania, which, with the help of greatly advanced archaeological sciences, ultimately pointed conclusively to the very opposite of what he had set out to prove. Polynesians came from the east, from the lower outposts of Asia via the islands now referred to as Melanesia, and eventually by great ocean voyages reached Tonga, Tahiti, the Cook Islands, the Hawaiian islands, Easter Island and lastly the islands of New Zealand, all now collectively referred to as Polynesia.

These Polynesians had managed, by way of their navigational skills and seafaring heritage, to populate this entire constellation of Pacific islands, isolated by vast tracts of the largest ocean on earth. Long before the first European explorers reached the Pacific, it had been mastered by the migrational feats of this ocean-orientated culture. Prior to AD 1500 the Polynesians were the most widely spread people on earth, a fact that did not pass unnoticed by the astute Captain Cook. 'It is extraordinary', he noted, 'that the same nation should have spread themselves over all the isles in this vast ocean from New Zealand to this island [Easter Island] which is almost a fourth part of the circumference of the Globe.' Even more extraordinary, in fact, considering they did so without the aid of any navigational tools or instruments. No compass. No sextant. How did they ever find these remote specks of land dotted around the Pacific? And, just as importantly, why did they attempt to do so in the first place?

It now seems from archaeological evidence that the Polynesians were often driven from their islands by overpopulation, famine or defeat in battle. In the style of true emigrants they would set off to make a new start. These voyages were planned many months in advance and conquering tribes would give the departing defeated enough time to build the massive double-hulled canoes that would eventually carry scores of people for eight weeks or more to their new destination. Once adrift, life for the community on board the platform straddling the hulls of the two ocean-going canoes would become a condensed version of life in the village. Men would fish, women would weave and attend to the domestic animals taken along for the new island home, whilst others dutifully bailed the hulls and maintained a continuous fire in the enclosed sand pit located in the middle of the platform. At night they slept, communally, under the scant protection of a small woven hut.

Following Mother Nature's clues the Polynesians were guided across fifteen million square miles of unknown ocean and by the 8th century they had colonized virtually every habitable speck on the Pacific.

In modern times, archaeology has given us the means to assemble and complete the picture of these Polynesian conquerors. In the artifacts, tools and weapons of everyday life, in the precious items of refined craftsmanship discovered all over the Pacific, and in the legacy of stone monuments such as those scattered around Easter Island lies the hard evidence of the common origins of these widely spread people. Their woodcarving, their stone adzes, their ornaments and their shell fishhooks all attest to their deserved reputation – in the words of Sir Peter Buck – as 'the Vikings of the Pacific'.

It is only fitting then that these courageous, heroic voyagers and conquerors should develop a strong tradition, almost a religion, of storytelling in a similar fashion

PREVIOUS PAGE (70)

**Koruru** *(gable mask). This Maori carving derives from the art tradition of central Polynesia. The Maori people shared the sacred belief that the artist was a vehicle through whom the gods created and communicated. Set in myth and tradition, carving was a sacred, honoured and cherished profession and, like all art forms in the South Pacific, it told a story of ancestral feats and legends.*

OPPOSITE PAGE

**Toki Pounamu** *(nephrite adze blade) made from the highly cherished green stone, nephrite (**Pounamu**), a geological relative of jade. Adzes were important woodcarving tools and a widely found Polynesian artifact. The rectangular section, ornamental in its beauty and quite practical in its application, is typically Polynesian. Exceptional skill would have been needed to make so refined a blade.*

FOLLOWING PAGES (74–75)

*In a graphic pattern that means 'welcome', a mat from a traditional community **marae** (meeting place) in what is known as the **taniko** weave serves to highlight the importance of weaving to Polynesian culture and society. Weaving is seen as much more than a manual skill. It is a vehicle that links the past to the present. Tradition and legend are drawn together by the weaver.*

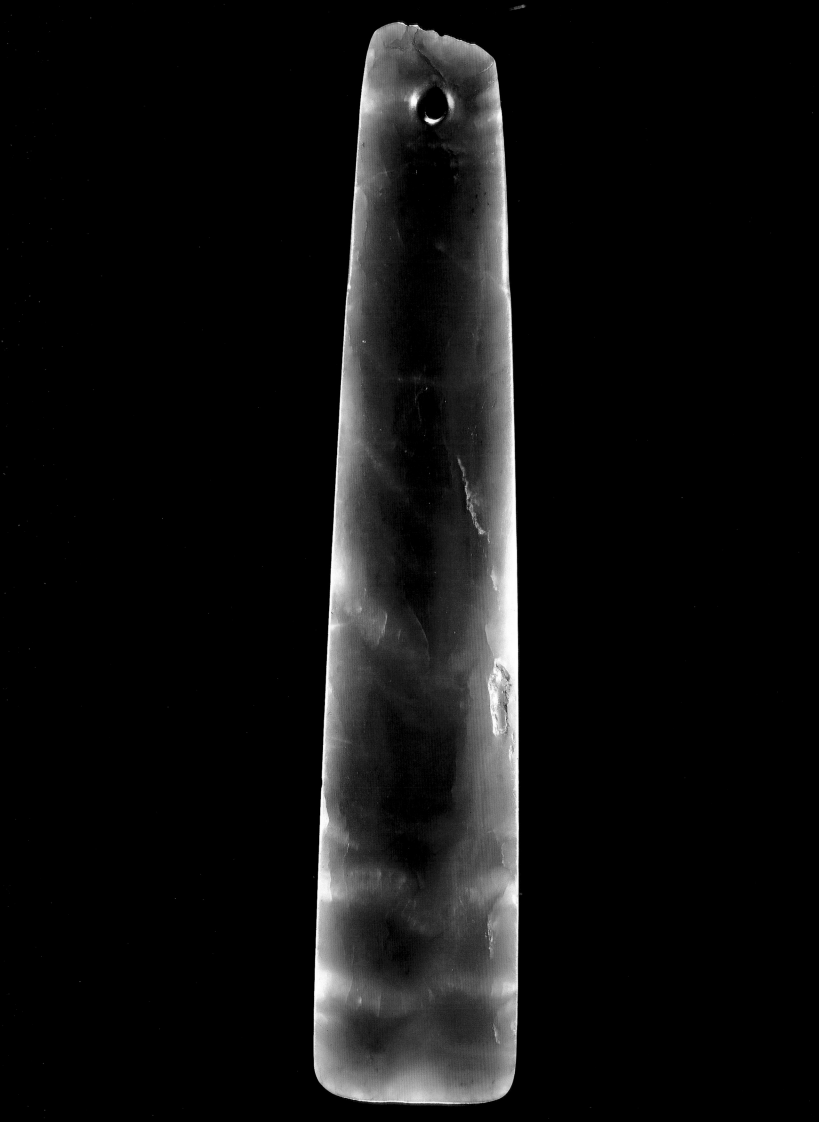

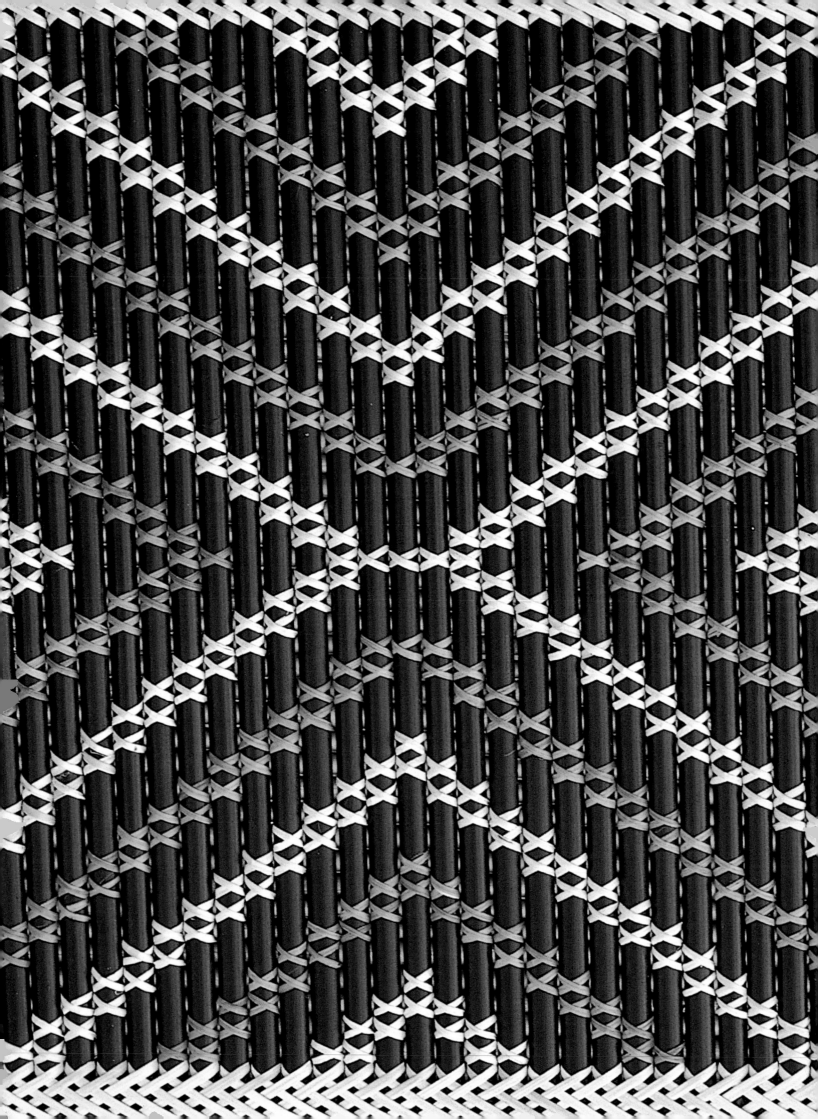

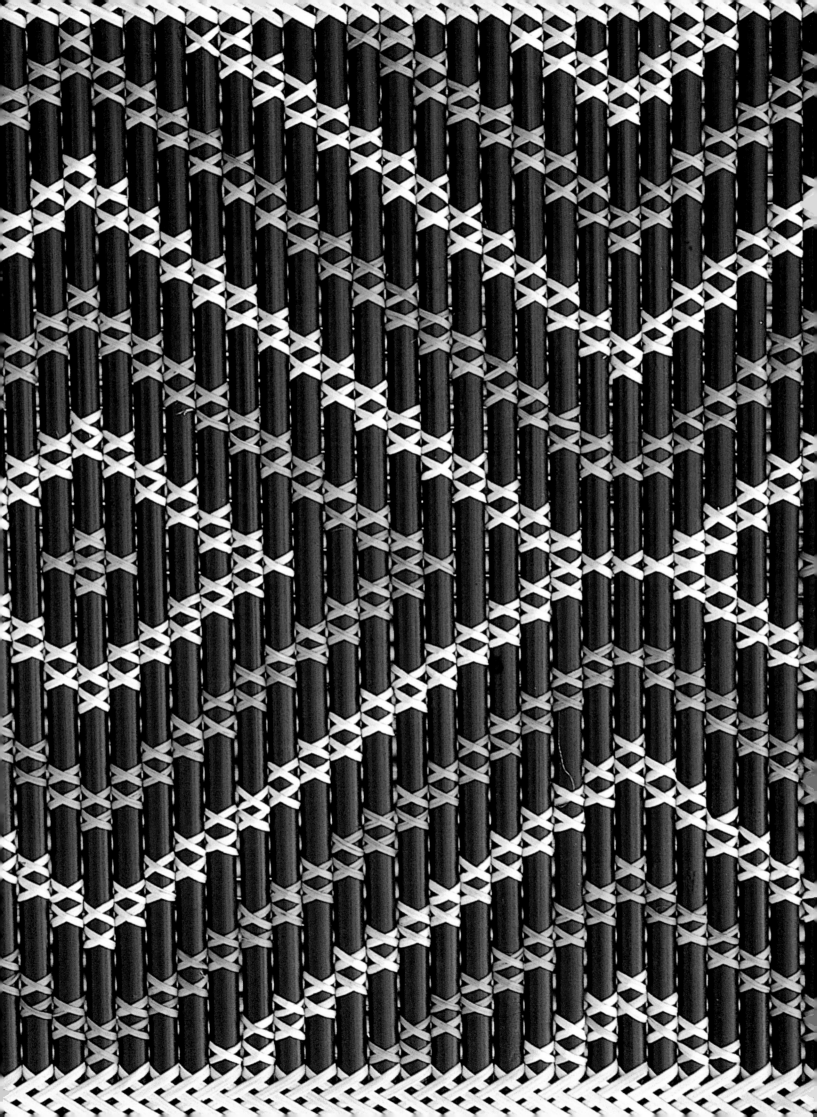

to their north European Viking counterparts. Legendary forefathers and heroic ancestors were worshipped and their tales told through all kinds of Polynesian creative expression. All Polynesian art and craft tells a story. The Pacific island traditions of timber carving, *tapa* cloth-making, tattooing and weaving are empowered with the mythology of their own genesis. Art is representative of the Polynesians' ancestry and as a result they love and respect it, just as they love their ancestors. Contrary to our way of life virtually everything they do is connected with a sense of spirituality. The things they create are meant to represent people of legend or ancestors who performed heroic feats … all this is recorded in their art.

For the Polynesians, *tapa* cloth, tattoo and carving perform the same function as community art and architecture in the Western world: they anchor the people. Art is their connection to the past and their continuity with the future. Art doesn't imitate life; it is life.

Today, this Polynesian culture continues through the modern translation and maintenance of these traditions. In New Zealand, Maori carving is still practised and the government is increasingly active in reintroducing the Maori language, an essential part of a culture based on oral tradition. On the island of Samoa, tattoo, the ancient ritual of body decoration, continues; on Tonga, weaving is still a revered tradition; in Fiji, *tapa* cloth is still made by the villages in a communal enterprise; and on the Cook Islands, traditional dance, another form of storytelling, is actively encouraged among younger generations.

Once threatened with extinction by the overpowering influence of Western colonial powers, Polynesian art − and thus Polynesian society − is returning to its origins and once again starting to navigate its own course.

OPPOSITE PAGE
*Hei tiki (neck pendant). Made of precious **Pounamu** (green-stone), the **Hei tiki** became an heirloom, gaining **Mana** (spiritual prestige) as it was handed down through the generations. These pieces of adornment were valuable status items because one's **Mana** was determined by one's heritage and roots. Before Christianity, ancestor worship was Polynesia's common religion. The Maori tradition of carving in greenstone continues*

*today with artists such as Hepi Maxwell, who produces pendants in the same shapes and symbols that have dominated Polynesian culture since before Europeans arrived.*

FOLLOWING PAGES (78–79)
*Samoan artist Fatu Feu'e has broken new ground as a Pacific artist by translating onto canvas images traditionally incorporated into Polynesian art forms such as **tapa** cloth, carving and tattooing. Feu'e, whose*

*adopted home is New Zealand, creates his work using Western techniques, but the forms, images and themes he refers to are rooted in Pacific chants, songs and legends. His grid drawings recall the composition of Samoan **siapo** (bark) patterns while his abstracted mask motifs are evocative of images represented throughout the Pacific. As Feu'e says, 'The only way to keep Polynesian art alive is to place it in a contemporary context.'*

# CORAL

# CHURCHES

## OF THE

## COOK ISLANDS

The European explorers, particularly those who came equipped for observation, such as Cook, Wallis and Bligh from England and Bougainville, La Pérouse and de Surville from France, were probably the last to behold a civilization of the Pacific as it will never be seen again.

With news of European discovery of the idyllic Pacific isles came trade, settlement, infectious diseases and other 'irresistible' Western influences. To quote Peter Bellwood, author of *The Polynesians*: 'A rather unbridled atmosphere of exploitation soon reduced Polynesian society and population to a shadow of its former self.' Where once Polynesians were regarded in learned circles as 'noble savages', survivors of a lost Golden Age, the gradual introduction of the seedier elements of European life seemed to confirm Rousseau's argument that 'it is, indeed, society that corrupts'.

The respect for the 'purity' of Polynesian culture was replaced by puritanical missionaries, who by the early 1800s had gained a substantial foothold throughout the Pacific. Dedicated to preaching a wholly inappropriate moral code to innocent and easily influenced islanders, they used an effective mix of gentleness and repression to create a 'bewildered and somewhat ashamed Polynesia' by the late 19th century. But not all that the missionaries did was destructive. They believed in land rights and helped the indigenous population fight for 'title' over and against the wishes of the European colonial powers that sent them in the first place.

They also contributed to an architectural legacy of sorts. Indoctrinated with a firm overriding belief in permanence, they sought to build 'houses of God' that could withstand even the force of the occasional hurricane. This was something the traditional *fare* (hut) definitely could not do and the islanders were greatly impressed by the power and permanence of these structures.

To achieve this solidity and durability, the missionaries chose to build in great slabs cut from coral. Whether or not they were aware at the time of the cultural significance of their choice, it was certainly a choice with cultural resonance. The famous trilithon monument Ha' Among-a on the island of Tonga, for example, was said to have been constructed about 1200 to symbolize the two sons of the ruling Tu i Tonga dynasty, and was built, as a ceremonial gateway, out of two impressive slabs of cut coral held upright by an equally massive crossbeam cut from the same material. In the monumental size of this piece one can also see shades of the monoliths that were to be cut from stone on Easter Island. Elsewhere, another monument, the burial mound of the Mu'a at Tongatapu, features stepped faces of cut coral leading in a pyramid style to a burial platform. Thus, the coral churches of the Cook Islands, intentionally or otherwise, followed significant cultural and historical precedents.

Cleverly, the sober, sombre outsides of these cut-coral structures completely belie what one finds inside. Their interiors bear an unmistakably Pacific signature. Although the form of these churches followed a rather uninspiring model – one, no doubt, taken straight from a typical village back in England – the islanders were allowed to choose the decoration and colour of the church interior, probably in order to keep the peace and encourage a greater rate of attendance.

In the most fascinating example of this creative 'pact', a church on Mauke Island in the Cook Islands was divided into two decorative halves as a peacemaking solution amongst rival villages.

The missionaries could not afford to build a separate church for each village, yet each community had a *Ta'unga* (master builder), who insisted on having the honour of building the house of God. Eventually, with no compromise being made by either

## "*English missionaries taught the Islanders to build.*

## *The Islanders, in turn, taught the Church a thing*

## *or two about colour.*"

PREVIOUS PAGE (80)
*A Gaudiesque sculptural form sits as an abstract insertion amongst flowering frangipani and coconut palms. This organic gate, framing the walkway to the church, is constructed from blocks of cut coral and topped with three crosses which are there to represent the highest ranking villagers.*

OPPOSITE PAGE
*Two **Ta'ungas** (master builders) from two separate villages each designed and decorated half a church. The half built by the **Ta'unga** from the village of Areora features load-bearing columns, which are painted in aqua blues, yellows, hot pinks and vivid greens, and has a roof structure that has been decorated with timber carvings.*

proud builder, the missionaries, in a flash of inspiration, decided on the Solomonic solution. Each village would be responsible for decorating one half of the church. The result is a truly fascinating interior. The church was divided down the middle, with the altar placed at the centre, and each village prepared its own pathway and set about decorating its own half.

Although the competitive animosity between the villages has long since disappeared, most people still abide by the separate entrances out of respect for tradition and their forebears, and the separate decorative approaches have been maintained. Interestingly, despite the fact that each village has chosen to go its own way, the two halves are remarkably similar. The split interior of the Mauke Island church is a monument to the strong cultural 'common ground' of the Pacific. Working with different forms and shapes, the two halves are, nevertheless, unmistakably from the Pacific. A strong communal sense of colour creates a uniform impression. The Mauke Island church is a *tour de force* in the use of indigenous pattern and colour.

On the Cook Islands, in particular, the old hand of traditional social structure fitted neatly into the new glove of Church hierarchy. Chiefs and family elders were replaced by ministers and deacons, and the sense of community hardly missed a beat.

During the 19th century, the London Missionary Society regulated life in the Cook Islands as if it were the government, uniting the people through a common faith and helping to keep the islands in native hands. Rarotonga, the main isle of the Cook Islands, was divided into five villages with a church at the centre of each.

One of these churches is of particular interest. It is the stately coral and limestone church of the village of Titikaveka, built in 1835. The oldest surviving coral church on the main island of Rarotonga, Betela, as it is named, is distinguished by its simple, symmetrically square construction, said to symbolize the equality of each person that

PREVIOUS PAGES (84–85)
*The Mauke Island church was built from blocks of cut coral rendered with a lime slurry, produced by firing unbroken coral in underground pits, a technique introduced by the first English missionaries. The strength and durability proved the* **Mana** *(spiritual prestige) of the Christian faith to the islanders.*

PREVIOUS PAGES (86–87)
*On the left-hand side of the photo is the half of the Mauke Island church with pitched roof designed by the* **Ta'unga** *(master builder) of the Areora village, and on the right-hand side of the photo is the vaulted ceiling that belongs to the half of the same church designed by the* **Ta'unga** *of the Ngatiarua people. A unique compilation*

*of aesthetics meeting directly above the pulpit, each half's contrasting design is linked together effectively by a uniformly riotous use of colour.*

OPPOSITE PAGE
*Pacific blue, bright yellow, emerald green and hot pink, the colours that Gauguin was accused of 'stealing from savages', unite a divided church.*

enters. It is one of the few churches that survives relatively unchanged. Set against pure whitewashed walls, a haunting shade that can best be described, rather predictably, as Pacific blue, has been used to decorate the elaborate and intricate structure that supports the roof. This impressive, interwoven structure is testimony to the building skills that are second nature to the islanders. Reminiscent of the organic designs of architects such as Gaudi, the interlocking posts, beams and rafters twist, curve and intersect like the intertwining vines of a jungle. When combined with the presence of Sunday parishioners, the church can make quite a strong visual impression. The regular male parishioners, dressed in black and white and standing together in one monochrome block, sing with gusto on one side, and on the other women in delicate, wide-brimmed woven hats and bright floral dresses answer the men's singing with soprano harmonies. Church is anything but a solemn occasion.

Although some might lament the loss of traditional Polynesian civilization, these coral churches of the Cook Islands have contributed an interesting new layer to the colourful culture of the Pacific.

PREVIOUS PAGES (90–91)
*The abundance of colour in the interior confounds expectations of what might lie beyond the stark formality of the whitewashed exterior. Running along either side of the vaulted ceiling that belongs to the Ngatiarua people's half of the church is a band of decoration that combines rhythmic repetition of colour and pattern with a powerful sense of symmetry. Variation is achieved in the scale and composition of the individual motifs which, because of their handcrafted quality, all differ subtly.*

OPPOSITE PAGE
*The interwoven timber roof structure of Titikaveka, the oldest and best preserved of the surviving churches built of coral in the Cook Islands, is a masterly*

*display of the kind of building skills that are second nature in these islands. Painted entirely in a single, stunning shade of Pacific blue, the structure is as ornate as it is strong. Intertwining like the vines in a jungle, the complex weave of support serves as a reminder of the Polynesian preference for organic shapes and forms.*

FOLLOWING PAGES (94–95)
*With its pure symmetry and simple geometric lines, Betela, as the church is named in Cook Island Maori, stands in quite pronounced contrast to its verdant, lush surroundings. Limewashed white walls, blue-painted Gothic window frames shipped to the islands last century by the London Missionary Society, weathered, exposed faces of blocks of coral stone and a*

*tidy, whitewashed and geometrically correct surrounding graveyard are all juxtaposed with the rampant green explosion of tropical island vegetation. Even the Bible, protected by a cover of woven Pandanus leaves, takes on different connotations when printed in the Polynesian language.*

FOLLOWING PAGES (96–97)
*In contrast to the dark, oppressive atmosphere of many Anglicized churches, the interior of Betela celebrates light, space and colour. Four square walls ensure a very un-Polynesian, non-hierarchical seating plan, yet ancestor-worship is still present: the six posts supporting the elaborate roof structure are each named in honour of the three highest-ranking mataiapo (villagers).*

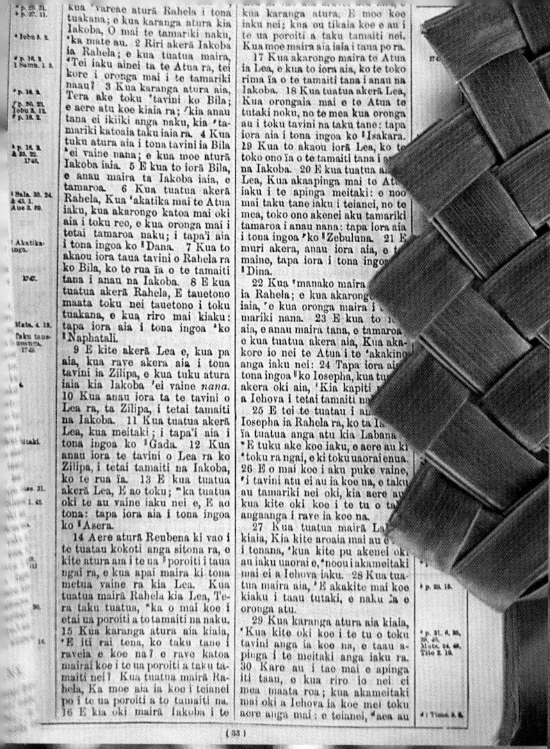
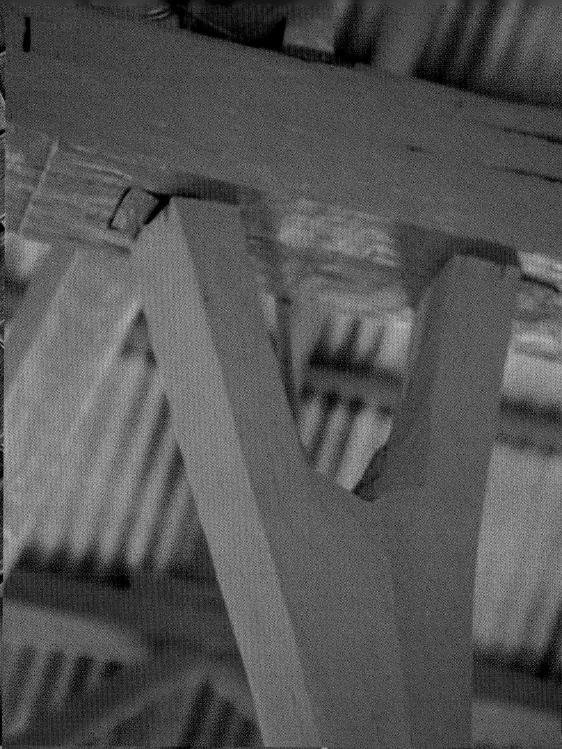
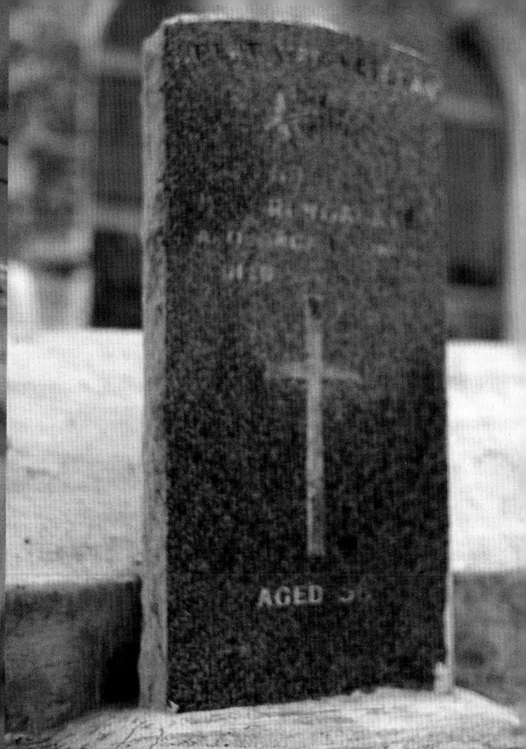
AGED
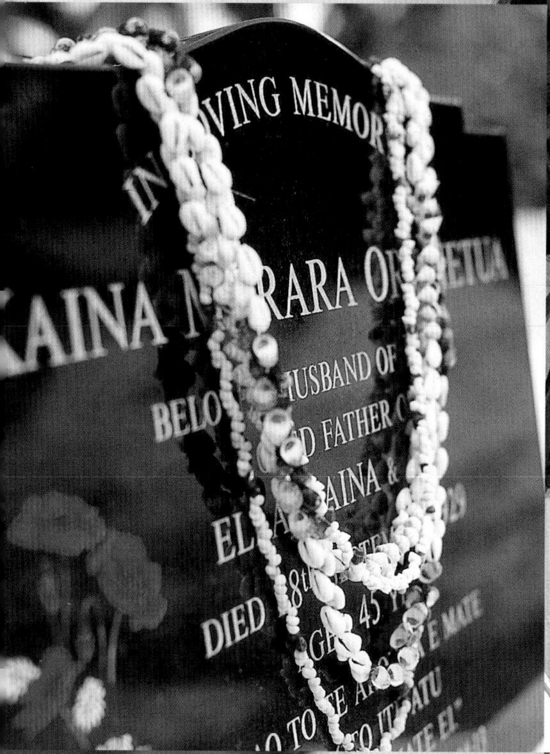
VING MEMOR
KAINA
RARA
HUSBAND OF
BELO
FATHER
DIED
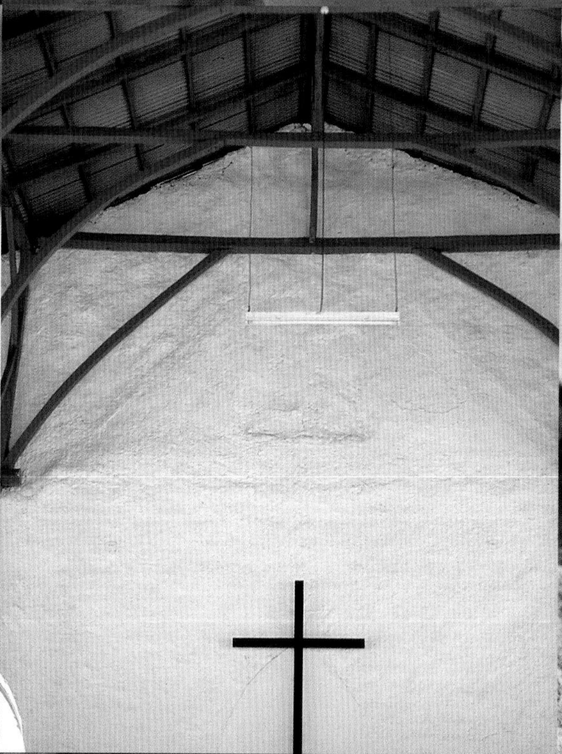
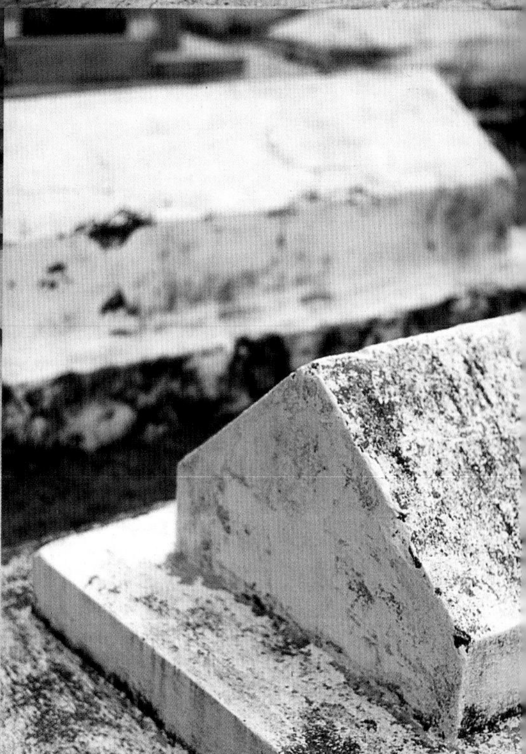
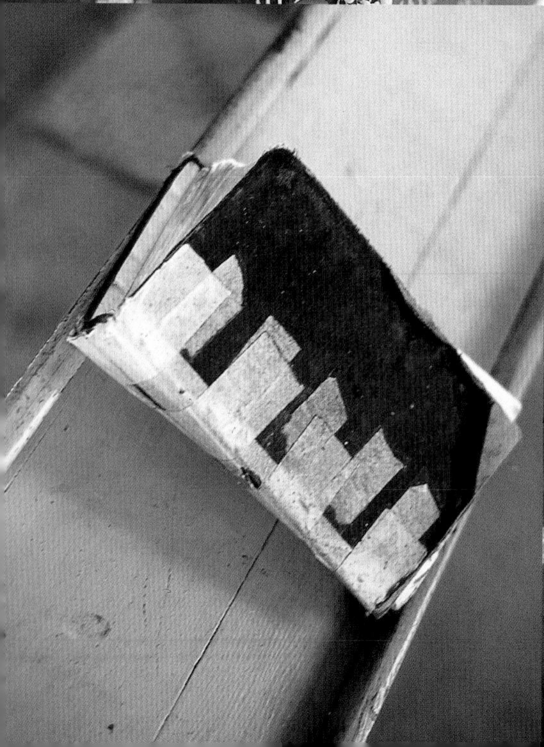
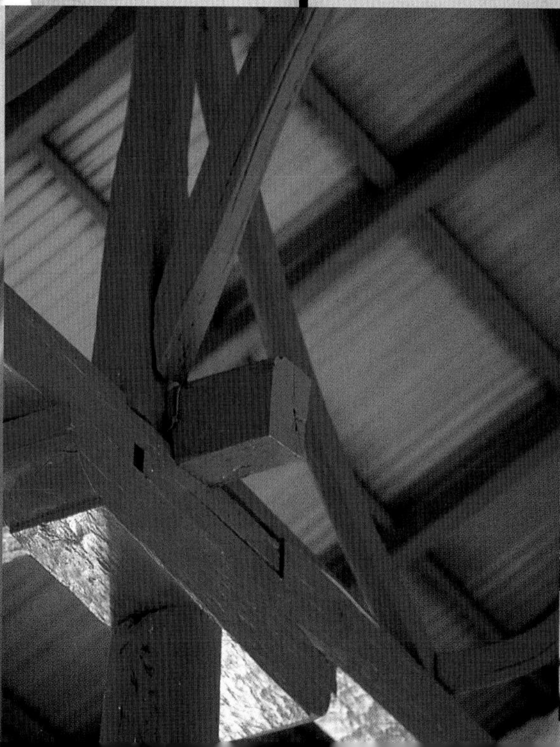
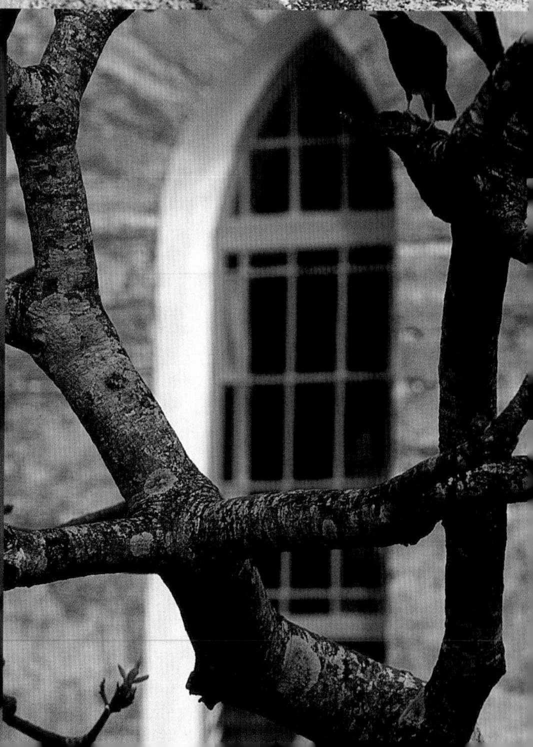

BETELA
ANNO DOMINI
1841, 1865, 1884, 1955, 1986

# 3

# COLOURS

*Colour plays a distinct role in shaping the visual culture of a city or country. It is one of the oldest forms of communication known, and we are attracted to it like magpies to a shiny object. Colour is simple and pure.*

# VIBRANT HUES

## OF THE

## SOUTH

# PACIFIC

Many of us first learn of the dazzling colours of the Pacific through the eyes of Gauguin. His canvases, painted in what were considered at the time 'impossibly' bright colours, inspire and bewitch with their intensity and power. Yet, ironically, the sense of colour for which Gauguin's work is celebrated was a remarkably simple and straightforward development in his career.

Having abandoned Europe in a quest for simplicity and fresh inspiration, Gauguin arrived in the Pacific with the same anxieties as most about the use of colour. However, once he had escaped the constrictive atmosphere of Papeete and found, as he had originally set out to do, the authentic Tahitian life and scenery, he discovered what the Polynesians already knew – that colour was simply an extension of life. As an artist he was finally able to submit to instinct. As he wrote in a letter: 'Everything about the countryside dazzled and blinded me. Coming as I did from Europe, I was always uncertain about this or that colour; I looked for difficulties where none existed. And yet it was so simple to paint things as I saw them, to put red or blue on my canvas.'

The colours that Gauguin chose to paint derived from the colours around him. Blue, Pacific blue, from the ocean and sky; green, the verdant shade of nature from the lush surroundings; pink, from frangipani blossoms; orange and yellow, the colours of tropical fruit such as pawpaw and mango. Here, on an island in the Pacific, Gauguin had discovered colour – the 'colours of creation'.

It was the Polynesian way. Pacific mythology had always recognized the sky, ocean and land as the most spiritual components in the Polynesians' own genesis; so colour, apart from being a natural choice, was also a spiritual choice. And this commitment to their own sense of colour has survived even the most concerted attempts by Europeans to introduce Western ways. Well-meaning missionaries may have succeeded in getting their female parishioners to 'cover up' in 'Mother Hubbards', dresses that conceal from above the neck to below the knees; however,

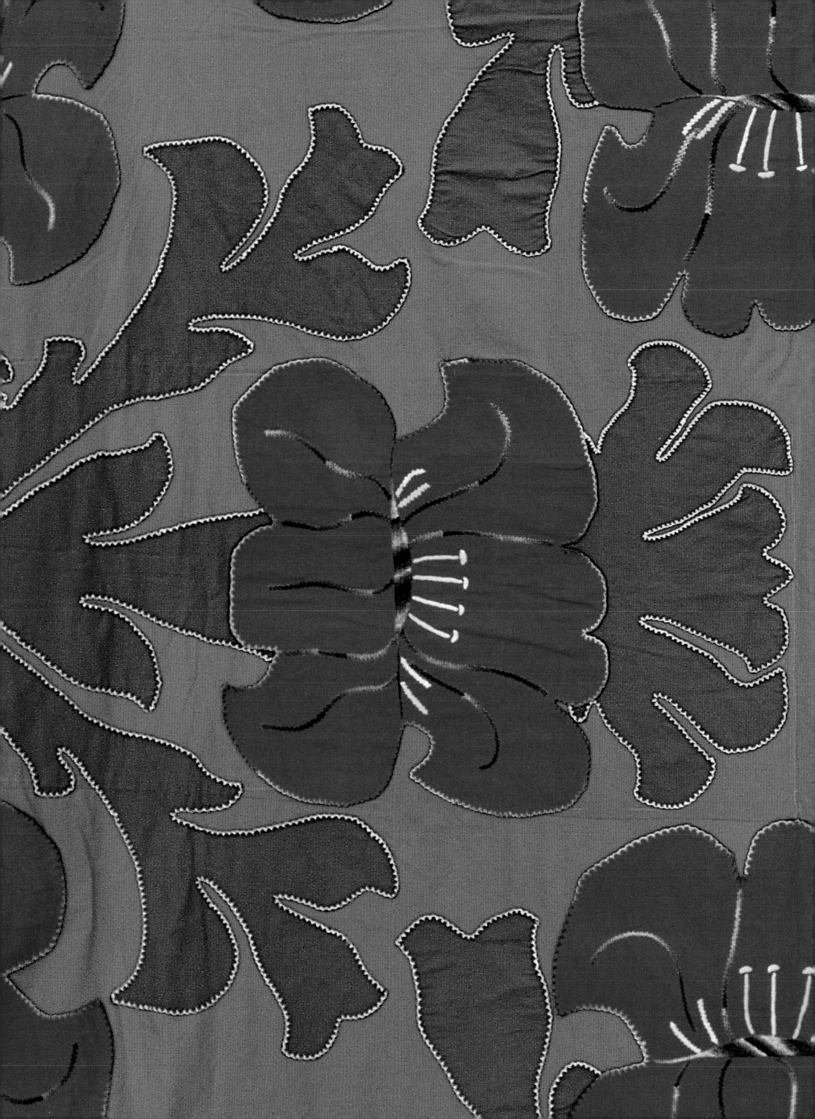

the preferred colours of these Victorian anachronisms, which are still being worn today, are the bright, unspoiled blues, reds, yellows, greens and pinks of Polynesia.

Plastics, polyesters and paint may also have found their way into Pacific life but they are still preferred in the shades of surrounding nature, colours that Gauguin referred to as the 'language of the listening eye'.

It is ironic, and a true indication of the extent to which we have been alienated from nature, that these colours, the colours of unspoiled surroundings, were until recently deemed in European circles to be too 'exotic' for public display.

*"Colour, which, like music, is vibration, captures that which is most general, and consequently, most elusive in nature: its inner force."*

Paul Gauguin

PREVIOUS PAGE (100)
*The colours of the Pacific are bright and pure and it is not difficult to trace their origins: a carved pillar of the Mauke Island church is painted blue – the colour of the sky, red – from hibiscus blossoms, and green – the colour of the land.*

PREVIOUS PAGES (102–103)
*Cook Island quilts combine the skills of patchwork, appliqué and embroidery. Taught to the islanders by the wives of missionaries, these joyous pieces of handiwork are distinguished by splashes of bright colour, representative of native flowers such as the hibiscus blossom, and set against the recurrent colours of nature.*

OPPOSITE PAGE
*Nature, the primary cultural influence and point of reference*

*for Polynesians, is reflected in their preference for colour. The colours they use are those of their surroundings – in this case, pink from frangipani and green from the forests. To encourage islanders to take an interest in the church, missionaries rather cleverly allowed them to decorate the interior.*

FOLLOWING PAGES (106–107)
*A church on the island of Rarotonga is decorated in subdued shades of blue with touches of yellow detailing. The church provides a firm social structure in the Pacific, and Sunday is the day on which the women of the villages get to show off the fruits of their fine weaving skills.*

FOLLOWING PAGES (108–109)
*Western influence seems to be inescapable, even in paradise.*

*Synthetics are used more and more; these plastic flowers adorn a church. The fondness for bright colour remains.*

FOLLOWING PAGES (110–111)
*A mat is woven from the leaves of the **Pandanus** – a plant found throughout the South Pacific. After soaking, the long leaves are hung out to dry before being cut into strips for weaving. Legend has it that Hina, the last cannibal woman of Rurutu, taught the women to weave shortly before she died of starvation because she steadfastly refused to eat anything but human flesh. **Pandanus** weaving is especially popular on Tonga, Polynesia's only surviving island kingdom, and decorative mats are worn on a variety of ceremonial occasions.*

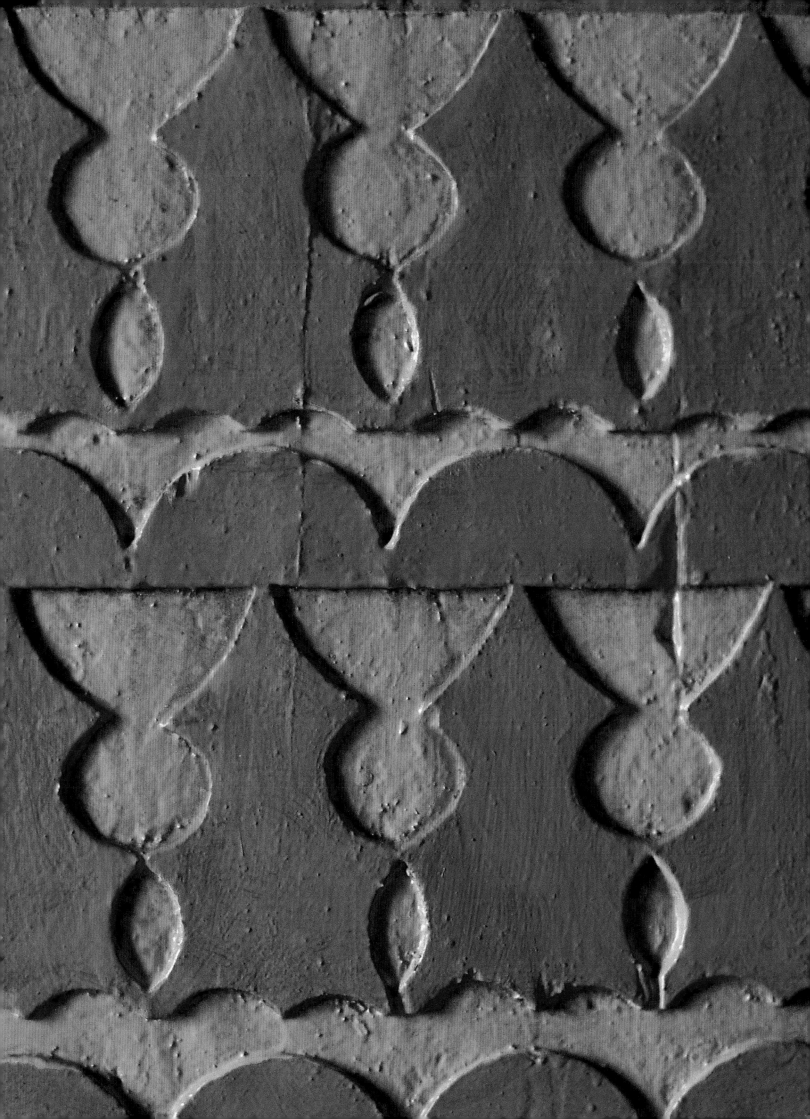

# 4

# INGREDIENTS

*Design is like a language. It is often specific to a place and its overall culture. The same symbols and patterns resurface in different forms and styles and they serve as both the source and the result of creative inspiration.*

# TATAU

## THE ORIGIN

### OF THE

# TATTOO

Tattoo, or *tatau*, originated in the South Pacific long before the first Europeans ever encountered an islander 'decorated with these distinct and permanent patterns'. Revered as an ancient Polynesian art form, tattoos are a badge of honour, a sign of courage, a testament of manhood, and they are prized possessions for which the islanders are prepared to endure months of agony. Tattoos form an important part of the social structure because, as with most South Pacific art, they tell stories about legendary ancestors and important chiefs, reinforcing the strongest cultural bond in Polynesia: that of common ancestry.

On Cook's first three voyages to Tahiti, the islanders were surprised at how seldom the Englishmen bathed, at their not plucking the hair from their armpits and how their naked torsos were devoid of any 'art'. Tattoos, which often decorated the buttocks of island women and the entire torsos of most men, were completely unknown to Europeans at the time. Often islanders would insist that their European visitors take off all their clothes, in spite of their protestations, so that they could identify which sex they were. This is how the Polynesians discovered, to their amazement, that Europeans did not decorate their bodies with ancestral stories and legends. Thus it was with these first voyagers to the Pacific that the practice of sailors being tattooed began. Even the aristocratic Banks returned to London sporting a small tattoo.

Tattoo, or *tatau*, as the first discoverers encountered it, survives today as a vibrant and spiritual Polynesian art form. Aside from the fascinatingly elaborate detail of these decorative expressions, it is the relationship of *tatau* to other Polynesian art forms that is particularly intriguing. For example, the characteristically rhythmic designs, composed of blocks of colour interspersed with geometric shapes and lines, closely correspond with the patterns found on *tapa* (bark) cloth. These recurrent motifs and symbols are the hallmark of Pacific art and they reinforce the important associations between different Pacific art forms.

Captain Cook, in particular, was fascinated by the precision with which tattoos were applied, especially considering the rudimentary nature of the tools being used. These consisted largely of sharpened and chiselled boars' tooths strapped to the ends of long sticks, which were dipped into a dye made from lamp soot and made to pierce the skin with a tapping motion. With one or two assistants to hold the skin taut, this slow and painful process could last several months. Cook asked Banks to sketch the tattooed face of a Maori warrior in order to record the perfect symmetry with which identical patterns had been applied to either half of his face.

Like all South Pacific art forms, *tatau* tells a story. Graphic geometric patterns converging across thighs and buttocks communicate legends of famous ancestors and tell tales that establish the place of their wearers in the world. In the hands of artists such as Samoan tattooist Su'a Suluape Paulo, this expression of Polynesian spirituality is enjoying a resurgence in popularity, particularly with the younger generation who are keen to emphasize their pride in their Pacific heritage. Not unlike other former colonial outposts, the islands of the Pacific are coming out from beneath the yoke of foreign rule and reasserting their own cultural heritage.

*"The woman must bear children*

*and the man must be tattooed."*

Polynesian proverb

PREVIOUS PAGE (114)
*At the time of Cook's first voyage to Tahiti, tattooing was unknown to Europeans. Many of the male Pacific Islanders whom Cook encountered had tattooed torsos, and it was thus that the practice of sailors being tattooed began.*

PREVIOUS PAGES (116–117)
*Often taking months to complete, the elaborate tattoos are realized with tools of sharpened boars' tusks and teeth, and with dyes made from lamp soot. Assistants hold the skin taut and sponge off excess blood during the long and painful process.*

OPPOSITE PAGE
*The characteristically rhythmic designs of **tatau** also reappear in other art forms, such as **tapa** (bark) cloth. The work of Su'a Suluape Paulo bears a striking resemblance to the **tapa** cloth patterns of Vatulele, as shown on page 67.*

*"An everlasting gem that you will take into your grave."*

From a traditional Polynesian song
about tattooing

# POLYNESIAN

## INFLUENCE

IN

## PACIFIC DESIGN

In 1893 Gauguin returned to France from his first journey to the Pacific and decided to compose an illustrated book entitled *Noa Noa* on the ancient culture of the Polynesians. It was, as he saw it, a way of helping people understand his paintings, designed for those who, in his own words, 'must always know the whys and where-fores'. With the aid of pen-and-ink and watercolour illustrations it told the story of the Areoi, and the world as created by these gods, believed to be resident on Bora Bora. *Noa* is the Polynesian word for fragrance and, according to ancient myth, fragrance was the first miracle of creation. Legend has it that this feat was followed by Le Tagaloa, the supreme god, rolling gigantic stones from the heavens into the sea to form islands. Flying clouds then married clear heavens to create offspring, including shadow, daylight and sunset. Creatures of the land and sea eventually gave rise to people, and chiefs were descended directly from gods.

At the time *Noa Noa* generated interest in some academic and artistic quarters, but it failed to bring a greater understanding of his new paintings to the art market. The world, and specifically the art world, it seemed, was not yet ready to accept Polynesian legend or culture as a valid inspiration and source of what was then considered to be 'real art'. Collectors deemed Gauguin's work too exotic and too caught up in the world of the South Sea Islanders. It was, they said, 'an art that did not belong to him … he was a civilized man, after all'. It was the first of Gauguin's many unsuccessful attempts to convince the art establishment of the merit and beauty of the Polynesian influence.

As with many of the world's ground-breaking artists, Gauguin was not to be given his due in his own lifetime. Yet he inspired a whole new generation of artists and, ultimately, he changed the course of art in the modern world. Gauguin's work paved the way for new and appropriate influences to be considered in the creative process. What was at first deemed too exotic became extraordinarily valuable. Polynesian

culture no longer has to be apologetic in its approach or to compete with European styles or standards. Designers, artists and architects in the Pacific now have a clear mandate to create with references familiar to their own culture, and they are actively doing so.

One such example is Humphrey Ikin's minimal furniture. Originally destined for a degree in economics, Auckland-based Ikin decided instead to pursue his belief that pieces of furniture can be cultural objects. In his opinion they can carry meaning in the same way as a painting or a piece of sculpture. The meaning Ikin refers to is implied rather than direct. His sideboard, for example, made from native New Zealand timbers, has a distinctly Polynesian 'feel' without any direct reference to Polynesian art or culture. It definitely belongs to the Pacific, yet it is in no way a cliché.

The designs of Stephane Rondel respond in a similar sense. His 'pin-up' chair, made from copper-plated steel and woven rattan, reveals a host of qualities that can be seen to be distinctly Polynesian. The woven rattan seat recalls the widespread tradition of weaving found throughout the islands, especially the weaving of the naturally coloured *Pandanus* leaf mats. In form, the chair shows the Polynesian preference for the curved, organic shape. In fact, were one to flatten the back and seat of the 'pin-up', it would reveal a Polynesian pattern found in carving and other traditional art forms.

These pieces are examples of the fresh creativity that is emerging from the Pacific. Drawing on its cultural roots and acting with a clear sense of identity, Polynesia is asserting its independence and rightful place in the world of design.

PREVIOUS PAGE (122)
*Set against the silhouette of Rangitoto Island on Auckland's Waitemata harbour, Humphrey Ikin's sideboard, made from native New Zealand timbers, is concerned with the serving of food. In form it is a marriage of the large communal bowl of Polynesia (hence the curve in the shape) and the European sideboard.*

PREVIOUS PAGES (124–125)
*Juxtaposed against a double exposure of swaying palms seen from the English arched windows of the church at Titikaveka, the Maria Vase, designed by Stephen White and Paul Lee, derives its shape from* **kumara**, *the sweet potatoes that are cultivated throughout the islands of the South Pacific, and the* **punga** *fern frond, which was mistaken by the first visitors to the islands for a pepper because of its spiral shape and red colour. The vase, named after a client, encapsulates the organic forms of Pacific culture.*

OPPOSITE PAGE
*Stephane Rondel's 'pin-up', a stackable café chair made from copper-plated steel and woven cane, is photographed against a background of native 'cabbage trees', so named because Captain Cook and the early settlers after him ate the fronds of this lily palm and likened the taste to cabbage. Avoiding sharp edges and straight lines, Rondel's chair is created with a preference, common to South Pacific cultures, for natural materials and the curved shape.*

# 5

# VIRTUOSI

*In music, in art, in almost every human creative endeavour, there are always people who stand out, people whose achievements warrant focus and attention. They often establish new directions and create pioneering approaches; they are leaders – they are the virtuosi in their chosen field of expertise.*

# MAORI
# MODERN

### THE ARCHITECTURE OF

## ANDREW

## PATTERSON

Near the beach immortalized by the haunting vision of a grand piano standing precariously just outside the reach of the pounding surf is a landscape so majestic and monumentally rugged in its purity that it is hard to envisage the notion of any manmade structure being comfortable in these overpowering surroundings.

A two-hour drive from Auckland, Karekare, with its black sand beaches and its lush and dense green hillsides, is the area that director Jane Campion chose to film *The Piano*, her Gothic tale of the struggle of early immigrants with the power and isolation of the nature around them.

It is a recurring theme in New Zealand: from the time the Maoris first arrived in *Aotearoa* (which means 'land of the long white cloud') the physical landscape has commanded and enjoyed a respect bordering on worship from its inhabitants, which has continued to the present day. For the Maoris, the land has always been sacred and throughout their history it has been their main reason for going to war.

Land was, and still is, a dominant factor in Polynesian culture, and it is the primary consideration for Auckland architect Andrew Patterson. 'The New Zealand landscape envelops us,' he says, 'it invites us to nestle in it, to be enveloped in the bosom of her majesty.' While the wide-open spaces in neighbouring Australia invite structures that sit on top and look out, Patterson's approach to architecture is to try to make the building become one with the natural contours of the land, so that the surroundings are the dominant feature of the structure itself.

Respect for the land has certainly not resulted in an apologetic architecture – far from it. With daring and inspiration, Patterson is building in a manner that takes up the gauntlet nature has thrown down. Patterson and his clients are not intimidated by the sites on which they choose to build; in fact, Patterson almost sets out to give nature a run for its money, to answer monumentality with monumentality, beauty with beauty.

Perhaps the best example is his first. Winner of the New Zealand Young Architect of the Year Award (when Patterson was twenty-five), this house in Karekare was, from the outset, destined to be one of those very special instances where a unique set of factors combine to create a piece of architecture that survives the test of time. It is, as a friend of both architect and client has called it, a singular, magnificent gesture. It started with an unconventional client, a gifted, intelligent, rebellious individual, unafraid to issue an aesthetic challenge. Nigel Horrock, a schoolfriend of Patterson's and an unusual adventurer who, for many years, ran a rafting school in Nepal, was lucky enough to be able to purchase an ideal piece of land, an old sacred Maori site, from mountain-climbing legend Sir Edmund Hillary.

Hillary, a passionate protector of nature's most impressive creations, agreed to sell the land on condition that any house built on it respected the landscape and surroundings. Patterson and Horrock rose to the challenge, not with the fear of despoiling a beautiful site but with the idea of challenging the majesty of the site, of designing and building something even more powerful than the surroundings. The result makes it a close contest. Nestling like a jewel in the cleavage of the bosom offered by the folding landscape, the house fits snugly into the surroundings and is enveloped by the verdant countryside.

Built on a gigantic scale, the structure sits like a bridge over a gully that eventually unfolds into a valley further down. From a distance it is difficult to decide whether the surroundings of the house add to its beauty or whether the topography is accentuated by the house.

It was with this Karekare house that Patterson developed an approach that has become a distinct signature of his work. The structure of the house, straddling a space between two rounded hills and approachable only by a rutted mud and dirt

PREVIOUS PAGES (130 & 132–133) & OPPOSITE PAGE
*Andrew Patterson's designs incorporate sliding and folding shutters that allow the full impact of the surroundings to be felt in the house. The orientation of the site was decided only after architect and client had spent many afternoons observing the surroundings.*

FOLLOWING PAGES (136–137)
*Suspended between the natural curves of the landscape, the Karekare house, with Patterson's gigantic sliding shutters, brings the majestic countryside into the full width of the living room like a cinema screen.*

FOLLOWING PAGES (138–139)
*Poised on the edge of the open-ended living area, an old armchair is the owner's favourite spot to appreciate the beauty of the property he was lucky enough to be able to purchase from New Zealand climbing legend Sir Edmund Hillary.*

FOLLOWING PAGES (140–143)
*Dominated by a monumental fireplace, the one living area of the Karekare house is furnished with ancient Asian artifacts and an old rug the owner brought back from his time spent living in Nepal. The furniture throughout the house is simple and unpretentious.*

road (four-wheel drive only), is in essence a container that can be opened on all sides by sliding doors of massive proportions – visual gateways that allow the surroundings inside to an unprecedented extent. To call it a good view would be chronic understatement: the house is endowed with the necessary mechanisms to virtually dissolve the distinction between outside and inside. From an opening the size of a cinema screen, the west coast landscape 'plays' in all its glory for the duration of the daylight. A cinematic analogy is quite appropriate because one of Horrock's favourite pastimes is to sit at the edge of the open-ended living room in an old chair recycled from a rubbish dump and watch the glory of the untamed, unspoiled wilderness unfold before him.

Sceptics would say that Patterson's work, splendid as it is, is limited to isolated sites with glorious surroundings, but another Patterson house, completed a little more than two years ago, proves that his sensitivity to the land, to Maori legend and to Polynesian culture can also be applied to the most urban of situations.

For a client in the city centre, surrounded by lacklustre commercial buildings, Patterson turned to Maori heritage for a solution to matters of privacy and quality of life. As Sir Joseph Banks observed on his journey with Captain Cook on the first voyage of the *Endeavour*, the low-lying houses of the Maori were usually built around a central courtyard known as a *marae* and it was here that all activity normally took place. Constantly aware of the threat of warring tribes, these centres were traditionally protected by surrounding fencing, and it was from their Maori structures and traditions that Patterson took his design inspiration. From the outside, the house when closed has the appearance of an impervious 'shed' with no doors,

"*The importance of nature, paramount to the Polynesians,*

*is the focal point of his design.*"

OPPOSITE PAGE
*Distinct Polynesian features, such as the monolithic pillars surrounding the courtyard's swimming pool and the 'open-to-the-sky' design, are clearly visible, even when executed in the most contemporary of materials. Patterson's Summer*

*Street house refers to and 'updates' Maori tradition in a clever and inventive manner.*

FOLLOWING PAGES (146–147)
*In complete contrast to the green design for which Andrew Patterson is well known, he has also demonstrated that his*

*sensitivity to Maori culture can work just as effectively in an urban environment. A house in the city uses modern materials such as aluminium to create an enclosed **marae**. A pivoting wall swings open to reveal the communal courtyard.*

windows or openings of any description … a fortress in aluminium planking. A few planks, however, constitute a hinged panel that creates an opening to the seemingly impervious façade and simultaneously serves as entry way and front porch.

Immediately upon gaining entry, the unwelcoming façade leads to a large central courtyard open to the sky, with a swimming pool in the middle and a series of monolithic structures, also very much part of Polynesian tradition, standing guard around this 'modern *marae*'. Maori mythology and modern reality blend very well in this house and the inspiration, although expressed in totally contemporary terms, is unmistakably Polynesian. This work, in particular, brings to mind Le Corbusier's thoughts on what it meant to him to be modern: 'To be modern is not a fashion, it is a state. It is necessary to understand history, and he who understands history knows how to find continuity between that which was, that which is, and that which will be.'

Since completing the Karekare house and the modern *marae*, Andrew Patterson has gone on to produce a series of other houses which share an approach that is distinct and similar, yet each time the buildings that result bear little resemblance to each other. The common thread is in the approach, not the form; Patterson prefers the site to be the hero.

For a beach house on Waiheke Island, an idyllic South Seas setting on the more protected east coast of Auckland's natural harbour, he designed an L-shaped 'shack' that is mainly concerned with bringing the beach, the palm trees and the green-blue ocean into the house as much as possible. It is a house without doors, windows or walls – or at least that's the way it feels. The entire structure is built, casually, on one big 'deck', which continues unimpeded to the edge of the ocean and the far ends of

OPPOSITE PAGE

*Sheltered from Antarctic storms by the mountain range that divides the northern island of New Zealand, the east-facing coast of Waiheke Island is soft, white, balmy and pretty in a South Pacific way. To be able to enjoy the island lifestyle fully, Andrew Patterson designed a house without walls or a roof, with a long arm of* **Mati** *timber decking that goes out to a palm tree and skirts the edge of a sand dune above the water.*

FOLLOWING PAGES (150–155)

*Andrew Patterson's most powerful design signature is his response to location. In the case of this Waiheke Island beach house, the position could not be better in order to enjoy the sea, sun and views. It had, as he says, 'good bones'. His response to this site was to allow it to be the hero. Weather permitting, the architecture virtually disappears, leaving only the enveloping beauty of the location. As he says: 'There is something about*

*the land that makes you become part of it; to dig in, to nestle into the landscape; to fold it around you.' As with the Karekare house, the use of large expanses of timber decking and sliding doors creates a peaceful, aesthetically pleasing line that leads one's eye out to the perimeters of the decking. It is a design that allows one to live fully outdoors, constantly aware of the ocean and always retaining a sense of being on one of the Pacific Islands.*

the house. The success of this architectural response to surroundings is a mechanism that, as with the house at Karekare, allows the house to open like a clever piece of origami. A curved track that suspends hinged doors, which can fold away and disappear altogether, allows the entire ocean-facing façade to be opened up in summer and, in reverse, to be closed to the elements in winter.

This is unpretentious, appropriate architecture at its best. Patterson is not concerned with influencing his clients' selection of furniture or their decorative preferences because, ultimately, he knows that all will be overpowered by the view. He has filled the interior with the surrounding exterior and nothing can detract from that.

At the time of going to press, Patterson was in the process of completing what may be his most striking project to date. Situated on a precarious peak, surrounded by black sand beaches, churning surf and verdant green, it exemplifies his notion of 'nestling into the landscape'.

Featured on pages 130, 132, 133 and 134, this 'Bethnells Beach' house cannot possibly compete with the surroundings and it doesn't try. Patterson is content, on this occasion, to design for his client the best possible venue from which to enjoy the spectacle of nature's performance.

When one thinks of Polynesia the mind drifts automatically to Gauguin's idyllic and colourful impressions of the South Pacific. Gauguin went to the South Pacific in search of simplicity, to connect with nature and beauty, an inspiration and process that Andrew Patterson has architecturally taken to heart.

# ACKNOWLEDGMENTS

*There is without a doubt an energy, vitality and commitment to Polynesian culture amongst the people of this region that has made a significant contribution to this book becoming a reality. In particular I owe many thanks to **Debra Millar** both for her intellectual and visual input. Together with photographer **Patrick Reynolds** she did a superb job of fulfilling her commission to photograph the extraordinary churches of the Cook Islands. In addition, Debra used her substantial knowledge and contacts on cultural matters of the Pacific Islands to ensure that no stone was left unturned in our coverage of the region.*

*I would also like to thank **Willem Rethmeier**, outstanding photographer and long-time friend, for his keen eye and talent for capturing the colourful essence of present-day Polynesia, and for his willingness to travel to remote places in pursuit of that powerful imagery.*

*In the same spirit photographer **Glenn Jowitt** travelled – sometimes even by canoe – to the far reaches of the Cook Island atoll to be able to capture precious moments of Polynesian culture.*

*From a design point of view I owe a lot to **Jan Heinen** and the design team at **Kader**, who helped create the basic graphic structure for this project. I am also indebted to the staff of **Thames and Hudson** for their advice and guidance.*

# PHOTOGRAPHY CREDITS

**Patrick Reynolds** *pp. 2–3, 12, 14, 42, 44–45, 46, 48–49, 68, 80, 83, 84–85, 86–87, 88, 90–91, 93, 94–95, 96–97, 98, 100, 102–103, 105, 112, 124, 128, 134, 145, 146–147, 158–159 (photos 4 & 5);* **Willem Rethmeier** *pp. 4–5, 8, 24, 26–27, 29, 30, 33, 34–35, 37, 38–39, 40–41, 50, 52, 55, 56–57, 58–59, 60, 62–63, 64–65, 67, 74–75, 130, 132–133, 148, 150–151, 152–153, 154–155, 158–159 (photos 3, 7 & 9);* **Mark Smith** *pp. 16, 18, 20–21, 23;* **Glenn Jowitt** *pp. 106–107, 108–109, 110–111.*

*The author and publisher would also like to acknowledge the following:*
*Artist Su'a Suluape Paulo pp. 114, 116–117, 119, 120; Haru Sameshima pp. 122, 127, 158–159 (photos 1 & 8); Greg Wilding pp. 6–7; artist Fatu Feu'e pp. 78–79, 158–9 (photo 6); Tim Rainger pp. 136–137, 138–139, 140–141, 142–143; Te Papa Tongarewa (Museum of New Zealand) pp. 70, 73, 77; © Stephen White and Paul Lee p. 125; © Diana Firth pp. 158–159 (photo 2).*

# BIBLIOGRAPHY

ALLEN, O. 1980. *The Pacific Navigators.* Amsterdam, Time-Life Books.

BAHN, P. AND J. FLENLEY. 1992. *Easter Island, Earth Island.* London, Thames and Hudson.

BARROW, T. 1979. *The Art of Tahiti.* London, Thames and Hudson.

BELLWOOD, P. 1978. *The Polynesians.* London, Thames and Hudson. Revised paperback edition 1987.

CACHIN, F. 1992. *Gauguin: The Quest for Paradise.* London, Thames and Hudson.

FISHER, R., E.C. LEE AND G.S. STUART. 1985. *Blue Horizons: Paradise Isles of the Pacific.* Washington, D.C., National Geographic Society.

GARDINER, M. 1987. *Footprints on Malekula.* London, Free Association Books. Originally published by The Salamander Press, Edinburgh.

GOLDWATER, R. 1985. *Gauguin.* London, Thames and Hudson. A concise edition of Robert Goldwater's *Gauguin,* originally published in 1957.

HEYERDAHL, T. 1950. *The Kon-Tiki Expedition.* Oslo, Gyldendal Norsk Forlag.

PEARCE, G.L. 1968. *The Story of the Maori People.* Auckland, William Collins.

*Taonga Maori.* 1989. Sydney, Australian Museum. First published by the National Museum of New Zealand.